AMAZING MILITARY FACTS

AMAZING U.S. ARMY FACTS

by Mandy R. Marx

CAPSTONE PRESS
a capstone imprint

le Plus is published by Capstone Press,
Roe Crest Drive, North Mankato, Minnesota 56003
v.mycapstone.com

Library of Congress Cataloging-in-Publication Data
Names: Marx, Mandy R., author.
Title: Amazing U.S. Army facts / by Mandy R. Marx.
Other titles: Amazing United States Army facts
Description: North Mankato, Minnesota : Capstone Press, 2017. | Series:
  Pebble plus. Amazing military facts | Includes bibliographical references
  and index. | Audience: Age 4-8. | Audience: Grades K-3.
Identifiers: LCCN 2016016906| ISBN 9781515709534 (library binding) |
ISBN 9781515709855 (pbk.) | ISBN 9781515711209 (ebook (pdf)
Subjects: LCSH: United States. Army—Juvenile literature.
Classification: LCC UA25 .M365 2017 | DDC 355.00973—dc23
LC record available at https://lccn.loc.gov/2016016906

Editorial Credits
Kayla Rossow, designer; Jo Miller, media researcher; Kathy McColley, production specialist

Photo Credits
Getty Images: Bettmann, 5; Newscom: ZUMA Press/Sgt. Daniel Cole, 7; Shutterstock: Radiokafka, 23, 24;
U.S. Air Force photo by Airman 1st Class Matthew Brunch, 13; U.S. Army photo by 7th Army Joint
Multinational Training Command, 15, Capt. Allie Payne, 9, Sgt. Ken Scar, 21, Sgt. Michael J. MacLeod, cover,
Spc. John Cress Jr., 17, Staff Sgt. Teddy Wade, 11, Visual Information Specialist Markus Rauchenberger, 19;
U.S. Navy photo by PH3 Shawn Hussong, 1

Note to Parents and Teachers

The Amazing Military Facts set supports national curriculum standards for science related
to science, technology, and society. This book describes and illustrates amazing facts
about the United States Army. The images support early readers in understanding the
text. The repetition of words and phrases helps early readers learn new words. This book
also introduces early readers to subject-specific vocabulary words, which are defined in
the Glossary section. Early readers may need assistance to read some words and to use
the Table of Contents, Glossary, Read More, Internet Sites, Critical Thinking Using the
Common Core, and Index sections of the book.

Printed and bound in the USA.
012017 010242R

Table of Contents

Amazing Soldier Facts

Army soldiers are brave fighters. The Medal of Honor awards bravery in the U.S. military. It was first given in 1861. Since then, more than 3,400 Army soldiers have earned one.

General Arthur MacArthur Jr. earned a Medal of Honor. He fought for the Union during the American Civil War.

A soldier's supplies cost about $5,000. This includes body armor, a gas mask, and night-vision goggles.

Amazing On-the-Job Facts

Dogs can serve in the Army.

The program is called the K-9 Corps.

Seven breeds of dogs can train

for service. The German shepherd

is a popular military dog.

All soldiers train to fight.
They also choose from
150 other jobs. Some soldiers
are doctors. Others do police work.
Some play in the military band.

Special Operations soldiers
have dangerous missions.
They sneak behind enemy lines
and rescue prisoners.
They capture enemies.

Amazing Vehicle Facts

The Abrams tank weighs as much as 10 male African elephants. Soldiers call it "The Beast."

The Boeing CH-47 Chinook

is the Army's largest helicopter.

It carries up to 33 soldiers.

It also hauls all of their equipment.

Amazing Weapons Facts

Many soldiers use the M4 rifle.

This gun shoots 700 to

950 bullets per minute.

That is 11 to 16 shots per second.

Other soldiers use the M16 rifle.
It hits targets up to 601 yards
(550 meters) away. That is about
six football fields.

Glossary

armor—a protective covering worn by soldiers

bravery—having courage

breed—a certain kind of animal within an animal group

capture—to catch and hold

corps—a group of individuals acting together or doing the same thing

equipment—the machines and tools needed for a job or an activity

gas mask—a mask that fits over the whole face to keep a person from breaking poisonous gas

helicopter—aircraft that can take off and land straight up and down

mission—a planned job or task

night-vision goggles—special glasses that fit tight around the eyes and help soldiers see in the dark

rifle—a long-barreled gun that is fired from the shoulder

Read More

Abramovitz, Melissa. *Military Trucks*. Military Machines. North Mankato, Minn.: Capstone Press, 2012.

Garnett, Sammie, and Jerry Pallotta. *U.S. Army Alphabet Book*. Boston: Bald Eagle Books, 2012.

Green, Michael. *The United States Army*. U.S. Military Forces. North Mankato, Minn.: Capstone Press, 2013

Internet Sites

FactHound offers a safe, fun way to find Internet sites related to this book. All of the sites on FactHound have been researched by our staff.

Here's all you do:

Visit *www.facthound.com*

Type in this code: 9781515709534

 Super-cool stuff!

Check out projects, games and lots more at
www.capstonekids.com

23

Critical Thinking
Using the Common Core

1. How might a gas mask help a soldier? (Integration of Knowledge and Ideas)

2. In what situations might a helicopter be more useful than an airplane? (Integration of Knowledge and Ideas)

Index